FREE FLOW

Kalisha D. Lemmitt-Cherry

PARENTAL
ADVISORY
EXPLICIT CONTENT

21&Up

Author: Kalisha D. Lemmitt-Cherry
Arranger: Peter Cherry, Kalisha D. Lemmitt-Cherry
Editors: Peter Cherry, Kalisha D. Lemmitt-Cherry
Graphic Designers: Peter Cherry, Kalisha D. Lemmitt-Cherry
Cover Art Director and Creator: Peter Cherry
Cover Concept: Kalisha D. Lemmitt-Cherry
Handmade jewelry, artwork and purse design by Kalisha D. Lemmitt-Cherry; coypyrighted and trademarked by by Angelic Reign Inc. Publisher; Angel Concept and Angel Logo by Peter Cherry, Angelic Reign Inc. ® 2004
ISBN: 979-8-9902578-3-2 Published and

Table of Contents

Hello and Hi

See a glimpse into my life experiences.
This is my journey good, bad, or indifferent.
Witness the beauty, the regeneration; with no apologies.
I may bring someone joy or pain.
Who said you wouldn't get wet from walking in the rain?
Living versus existing should be educated
and debated subjects for change.
Ideas and images changed to protect
those people, places,
or things.
Some will read to be nosy,
but those who read it will know me, or
know me better.
I'm writing this like an open letter.
If you want the whole truth; well, here's my story.
I may speak what one can't or won't say.
You're looking down the barrel
of my intellectual shotgun anyway.
I hope I didn't scare you away.
Thank you for traveling, and moving this way.

Kee Changes

From hard work to hardly working,
some just don't understand.
What is in the master plan, or flim-flam scam?
Can you point me in the direction
of humanity that gives a damn?!
Generating a regeneration of a nation
full of upsetsand greed.
Good or bad, sometimes we are all that we need.
When working hard towards your goals,
you can never be defeated.
Love, inspiration, and motivation.
Here comes the changes.
Plus, harmony and patience,
are essentially the keys to things that are needed.

Lady Grit

Can't keep up with this bullshit upon foolishness;
funky attitudes being rude.
Just find another way.
Don't thrive always on struggle issues,
becoming uncaring,
self-absorbing; deflecting the truth every day.
Sometimes, people do it to themselves.
If a flower can grow from manure,
you can grow from others and their shit.
Question: "What part belongs to you?"
Truth should benefit all actions and intentions.

Thought

The world keeps spinning, and life keeps changing.
We continue to move forward and progress.
At times, it can be hard and scary.
We worry and want, while trying to make sure we take care of our needs and others.
We try to sleep when we can.
Have fun when it is possible.
Try to love to the fullest.
On our worse days, we are better.
Our structure and minds were built to sustain.
Our truth, faith, and love will always remain.

Want List

What do I want?
What I want is to have a peace of mind.
I want to
continue to live in the present state of mines.
I want to
progress and process everything.
I want to
continue to love and be loved.
I want to
continue to be healthy and happy.
I want to
continue to be financially fit and flexible.
Most importantly,
be myself;
finding new ways to discover who I am.
Continue with showing
love and appreciation to everyone.
While kicking society's anxiety in the ass.
Lord,
I want clarity for me…
the sheer…Simplicity (I'm cool with that).

Inner Peace

Sometimes you have to separate yourself from some people, places, and things.
How much time are you willing to spend with yourself?
Self-worth is the best prize.
You have energy for others; but, for yourself, you just do not.
Love comes close, or at a distance to those.
Gifts worth far more than earthly treasures and riches.
You cannot afford to deny yourself.
It depends on what direction you take with yourself.
Have you fully learned yourself?
Have you fully experienced life, or
such peace as you would like?
Is it what you were blessed with Yourself?

Patches

Just a misfit trying not to get played like a toy.
In the attic of your mind, I'm confused;
is this my mind or yours?
"Yep, I'm out there."
A misfit indeed.
'You're out there.'
'A different, intricate, and delicate patch, indeed.'
Listen to me.
You always said your blessing were
yours, and not meant for others.
What is it that makes you so different from others?
'You are from the same cloth, but you
cut yourself away.'
Rejections and unannounced affirmations
have been delayed.
'They cool until they ain't cool no
more,' is the use-them up craze.
Damn, I said I wanted to be open and honest.
You wonder if all of this is true, and a
misfit of patches, is you?
My gems of wisdom don't make them
money or happy.
Nobody or nothing seems to; they ain't it no more.
Cursing themselves upon silks of self-
rejection and deflection.
Why should I still dedicate the time to
others that aren't even worth a piece of my time?
They still somehow come across my mind.
I was once just a misfit of patches that
got tailored made for goodness.
I try to be open to receive; but not be deceived.
We are patches in God's eyes.

Go-als

Generally, speaking…fuck the haters!
Don't worry about what they will say or not say.
The first two letters of goal spells, 'Go.'
Go receive that message.
Go get those blessings.
Go where others will not.
Your goals are what make you unique.
Everyone may not share or even understand that goal,
but you should not let that stop you.
Go get what's yours.

INSOMNIA

I'm so sleepy…
Well, SLEEP then!
Come, take me away.
Put me to bed.
Give me you; pillows; and blankets!
I'm so tired; I want to sleep!
But sleep eludes me…
I am wide awake…again,
listening to the heavy sleet on the roof.
Even the flameless candles have timed out.
INSOMNIA.
Snores drift next to me; a sweet lullaby to me;
but I am still awake…
I do envy that sound…
I'm up with the night crew; clubbers, and cat walks.
Am I just a sleepy head in need of a bed?
INSOMNIA.
See, insomnia is a bitch waiting for you in the dark.
Creeping and snatching your sleep,
like a five-dollar wig being snatched off your back.
Staring at the ceiling;
while the sound next to me is asleep.
I am shaking my head for thoughts of disrupting
a slumber within my reach.
Fuck it!
Never mind as the birds starts to creak.
INSOMNIA.
Can't go back to sleep!
Might as well get up and get going…
Damn….

Chasing a Snooze

Time passes and does not wait.
Faithfully, it returns.
It moves quick or slow,
depending on your flow.
The routine is the same old, same old.
The route to get there has not changed.
Then, you are at a place where
too many people call your name.
Then, before you know it,
you are celebrating to leave;
maybe taking a cool ass nap; or even
forgetting that time exists.
Then, it is time to leave for the chain gang again.
Bang; bang goes the car doors.
Looking into the sky until my eyes fade;
praying for a peaceful and easy day.

The Weekend, Love

Fall in…
slowly…
rainy day…
hold me…
chocolate kisses...
you know me…
sleep in…
longer…
snoring…
getting stronger…
rain…
dropping harder…
Let's just sleep in this weekend.

DREAM

Totally asleep; no time to weep.
Falling deeply into an abyss of bliss,
I dream.
Further than the ground in front of me.
Further than the gulf of the sea.
Further than you and me.
I dreamed my dreams into a reality.
But after I feast,
I must relax and be at peace,
and continue to succeed.

Just Be

Life can have strife.
Love can be nice.
If things do not come today,
the world keeps turning.
God is the gatekeeper.
Be one with your faith.
Trust and relax in knowing who you are.
Dare not to pretend; be surprised.
Don't be defined by other's selfishness;
expectations; or ill actions.
Guard against those who are not for you.
Everyone has an asshole and that means:
"Breathe in, and roll your shoulders!
You are worth the wait!"
"Breathe out, looking with:
'Who the hell you think you talking to!'"
Within your eyes,
just be yourself.

Poetic License

I know what I mean, and speak what I want.
I can write it how I talk it.
Now please, walk away.
This is my poetic license,
my justice; actually, me!
This didn't just come from a degree.
I'm consistent, take the good or the bad.
Sometimes;
I don't like leaving conversations un-had.
Especially when your approach to me
is,"big and bad."

Fall back, pardon as I laugh.
You are so funny and corny.

Stop confusing yourself asking stupid ass
questions.
I said what I meant, and meant what I said.
So don't share your confusion with me.
I don't care if you didn't get it or understand.
What is it about my melanin, my gender,
my banter, that makes it so hard for you to
accept and understand?

Happy Thoughts

Happiness
is what you make it.
Some may not be
Happy
when you are
Happy.
But never, ever deny yourself your
Feelings and Blessings of being
Happy.
You can be
Happy with a little, or
Happy with a lot.
Some may try and make you feel bad;
like you cannot Smile and be
Happy;
or cannot express your
Happiness.
It is okay
to feel sympathy or empathy for people.
What is not okay
is for people to make you feel bad or
guilty because you are
Happy.
At times, it is easier to be mad than
Happy.
Do not let others bring you down.
It is not your fault they need certain things
and aspects in their lives in order to make them happy.
It is very fucked up when they wrong you,
but when they see that
YOU are the one that is Happy,
they may look at you with an attitude and ask,
"Why you are Happy?"
Just remember your stop to get off the mad hate train.
It is all about trying to have a balance.
"It's okay to be Happy!"

Issues

People are
going through something the same or similar.
Not everything is singular; but plural in the journeys.
A little bump in the road; some bruises from praying;
and some heartaches after pain.
Insanity pursues in the world and in your brain;
you feel like things ain't gonna change.
You race with your mind; and your heart skips along.
Please realize that you are not alone.
Definitely not by yourself.
Some people deal differently with stress.
Some chase wealth.
Others need medication/self-medicate.
Most ride the body wave; emotionally,
physically, mentally, and spiritually.
And, rest assured that you are not by yourself.
Family issues.
Health issues.
Addiction issues.
Relationship issues.
Money issues.
Education issues.
Food issues.
Sex issues.
Employment issues.
Weather issues.
Future issues.
Present issues.
Past issues.
Imaginary issues.
What the fuck issues.
We wear our issues like shoes.
Some just may cost more than others.
"You are not by yourself."

MAYBE

Today wasn't my day;
but it wasn't yours, either.
Maybe,
you should have come right and not left.
Maybe today is not your day;
but it will always be another day.
Another day will begin;
so, don't start with me.
The sunset will end.
One more day to lose or gain.
Days to have times well spent.
We do not know what the future holds.
We should not keep reliving the past.
Do not wait for better days.
Have a better day today.

Chamomile and Sunflower Seeds

'Chamomile is calmness; sleep is not normal.'
Brewing smoke is stress; it's too cold;
and ain't you too old?
Keep it cordial.
So good night is what I told the tea, while
pouring it so naturally.
I can spit rhymes like sunflower seeds.
Disrespect me, and I'll give you
what you never thought you would need.
Lyrically bringing them to their knees,
I make grown men turn bitch when I go beast.
Spitting what I flow from these sheets.
Chamomile and Sunflower Seeds.
Don't expect for anyone to understand.
This mind of mines is a goaled mind.
Still; don't expect for you to understand.
People need to realize,
the world is still full of fools, crooks, and thieves.
(You need me!)
Bitch…please; if that's what you believe or see.
I don't need you;
I shake you off like a flea.
That's just not for me.
I lace it up and continue on this
stride through my spirit and life.
No need for me to sprint to gain strength and pride.
I'm alive; just look into my eyes;
I've seen the past, and the future.
Thank you,
God for the present in advance.
Chamomile and Sunflower Seeds.

Don’t expect for anyone to really
understand this one.
This mind of mines is a goaled mind.
Still; don’t expect for you to understand.
Don’t deny me; you will always lie to me.
Hello; what can I do for you today?
Because you can’t do shit for Me!
You need to get focused,
and shut the fuck up.
My written flow so dope;
bursting out of the pages like,
“BOOM! What’s up!”
Chamomile and Sunflower Seeds.
I told you that you wouldn’t understand.
Hocus Pocus gotta get focused.
Have to spit knowledge to people
like sunflowers seeds.
Yes, chamomile is still calming.
But my mental health is almost exhausted.
Which is making me physically exhausted.
And emotionally, I can’t deal with people.
I won't let it mess with my spiritual health;
I need not wild out on people.
Chamomile and Sunflower Seeds.
Do you understand now?

Break

Some are just here for the comments.
“Let’s see what she wrote.”
"What meme did he post?"
"Who just had a baby?"
Some people post bullshit; funny papers;
and darkness online.
Yet, we tend to still
find our way to the comment sections.

Find Ass Section

Money can be the factor of all fallouts;
fights; and struggles in life.
Look at the way of the world today?
Can't get a pass without spending
time or money either way.
You may have too little, but make it work;
working at a job that does neither
appreciate nor pays you what you are worth.
You may have too much,
but want much more; but are in debt.
Living above your means trying to live
high on the horse is actually
hurting you more.
People may match or share with you,
but complain if they feel like they are doing more.
People may have enough, may have none,
and want to take some more.
People can, get in over their heads.
It's a pity just trying to make, take, or steal that bread.
Save your coins, work hard, increase your money.
Piggyback off your own piggybank.

Understand

I am not perfect, understand.
Finding a good soul is like looking
for a grain of rice in the sand.
Where are the people like me?
That try to listen, learn,
work it out and understand?
Don't laugh with me, then complain to others about me.
Understand.
Then complaining about others to me to make it
seem you just like me.
Understand.
Damn!
I know that there has to be
a few good people out there just like me.
I could go on and on,
but I will try not to do that to you.
Even if I do explain, it may not be worth it to you.
Understand.
Or, at least try to.
Especially when you know your heart and truth.
I am not tiredly righteous like
the others with bad intentions.
Understand.
My goodness can be good,
yet my honesty may have you start a sentence with a,
'But ……'
That is why I don't say too much.

BOOOM

When it's occupied with snakes and scallywags,
I dislike being in a room full of people and
their bad attitudes; it just reeks of boo-boo.
Being around them so much I have to leave
and go air out my mind, and shake them off me.
I would rather smell like strip club smoke.
At least I would know why I was there.
I feel like I need to run that back…
Meaning, what's your vice?
Like reading is not just for books.
I'm naughty and nice.
He wants to snack.
I want him to break my back.
No need to check the time, just get that check.
Sometimes I may wear my heart on my sleeve,
but keep my mind in check.
It's our season; asking you nicely to fall back.
I'm the leader of the pack.
You awoke the beasts; and later, we must feed.
Just let me breathe and roll;
don't wanna smell your stink.
Like cream, I have been rising to the top.
Just wanna party and shit;
don't wanna hurt anybody.
BUT please, don't test my nature!
You do so, and even the incarnate words
can't save ya!
While our heart is true; others are false;
and their auras are scummy.
They make me feel, ehh, and funny.
I am chewing and spitting you out like pork fat.
All this bullshit got my tummy hurting.
I'm so dope make the healthiest go ill.
Be careful, people, you will try to fight these rhymes,
but they kill.

My lyrics can help you sharpen up
your listening skills.
Me?
Ain't no half stepping!
Gotta keep moving; gotta keep progressing!
Ain’t no stopping;
I like walking in the rain.
Too much?
You paused; looked around and asked,
“Who was that?!”
Like you really want to know or be here.
Your attitude is stinking too badly;
and you need to get lost.
DYNAMITE DUO AIM for dreams
whatever the cost.
Ain’t hearing or feeling that shit.
While our hearts are true; others are false.
Everyone we see are a tad bit soft.
Let us make this dough; we’re always the boss.

Done Arguing with Ignorance

It is sad!
I got left out there!
How can I express how I feel when the person
I'm trying to express myself to don't listen!
I'm done!
I guess I just can't get it right!
Move one way that wasn't the way for others,
or how they wanted me to move.
Fuck all of you toxic vain ass fuckers!
In the past, I overlooked others
and their self-described faults;
and shared aspirations; insights,
feelings with them.
I just don't give a fuck now!
I didn't want to come from the left, but I guess
I was right all along.
"How it is and how it is supposed to be may vary."
They tell you, but they don't want you to speak.
They hear you, but they don't want to listen.
When they do, that doesn't mean that they
listened in the first place.
They are probably so busy in their head that
they only pick out words that either benefit or
deflect from others or even themselves.
"That's sad!"
They always seem to find their way back to hurt.

It looks like you did something to them,
and even if you didn’t or unintentionally,
it still doesn’t matter.
“I don't even think it was my fight in the first place.”
“Don't even think it was before…”
“It's not my fight anymore!”
Sometimes situations are bad, because it is bad,
and it is not what it is supposed to be.
You better look at the truth and just let the truth be!
Know the difference!
“Whatever; that is your stance; but this is my stance.”
God is good and has you.

BANANAS

It is crazy; it is insane.
What one thinks in their brain.
Can be sweet like sugar cane.
But I can snatch you down to your grains.
Then blow you up and make you go insane.
This is bananas.
This shit is bananas.
The day in a thought of you; me; or him.
Days of thoughts about we; who; and her.
They can't comprehend or know about
this shit right here.
This is bananas.
It is fucking bananas.
This is the greatness that geniuses stand for;
we have the crowd jamming,
waving their lighters, wanting more...
Stepping into adulthood and getting
older; thanking the Heavens.
Why be worried; and what for?
I know I can look in the mirror,
and I am proud of her.
This is bananas.

Dusty Mirror

"Where are you FREE?!"
"Good questions, and observations…"
When you are tired, the energy is just not there.
Please sit back and take the time for
YOU!
"Open your mind, and close your eyes."
Feel deep within yourself.
Take care of your
mental;
spiritual;
emotional;
and financial health.
Let yourself be free and clear.
Follow your mind to a calm place.
Take your spirit to a serene state.
"Loosen your soul."
"BE FREE!
Let it go!"
Those same people, places,
and things will be there tomorrow.
But they do not have to be in your world forever.
BE FREE!
Lose them…and find
Yourself.

Know

Only when you know what's behind you,
that you can plan for the now.
You always had this,
God has always had you.
You have to keep on progressing;
moving; and focusing on your main prize:
YOUR life.
So what if everyone's views are different.
You were created in God's likeness.

Working on It

I wish that...
I could say the things about people
that they seem to say to me.
I know and have been the truth on somethings.
BUT…
I try to have humanistic courtesy.
Of course, I am human.
I still grow to understand, not just myself more,
but people more.
I learned that with growth, people may or
may not be where I feel that I am or even trying to be.
I learned the everyone does not think like me,
but they also shouldn't feel the need to disregard or
use the fact of how I think against me.
Yea...
People don't listen to me;
or hear me until it benefits them.
My feelings are valid;
and a few people may say you think your better.
I said it from the door take this as an open letter.
I continue to grow and know that I am okay with that.
I continue to mature,
and make assessments and corrections.
I wish people would see that more.

“MEditation”

I meditate on a productive day of positive energy.
My energy is felt and spoken
out into the force of the universe.
I am open to the depth end of
my own feelings and emotions.
For my releasing; for being one within unfamiliarity;
but with familiarity understanding.
Expressing of one’s feelings showcases
one's growth inside out, and
without compromising my own; my integrity, and spirits.
The wisest are able to speak thoughts
and aspects within an empty space.
To fill the universe with love because it matters.

SERENITY

Serenity...
I meditate on a productive day
of energy;
for my releasing; for being one of the wisest
in the matters of a universe
filled with unfamiliarity.
My energy is felt and spoke out into the force.
The universe of familiarity understands,
because the expressing of one's
feelings showcases one's growth inside out.
I am able to speak about thoughts;
aspects that are triggered within the empty spaces.
I am open to the depth end
of one's feelings and emotions;
without compromising my own;
my integrity, and spirits.
I am being open to the depth of one's truth
that can only come from sleep;
prayer; fasting; talking; and meditation.
May I ask that the outcome be in my favors?
These blessings
ARE from my Lord and Savior…
SERENITY...

Backpack Cape

Always wore my backpack like a cape.
At any moment, I was ready for an escape.
Call me a bag lady…
I was ready to pack and go.
Too many ideas to contain;
too many moves to make; but I was keeping sane.
Running slow on energy, but fast on ideas.
It's simple; just trying to give you all a feel.
Mind's right; mine's tight; but now I gotta go.
On to the next adventure.

Sage of Grass

In need of solitude like Walden.
So, the Pond I seek.
The fall Of Leaves.
The Grass I sit.
I sit and ponder.
Which way to go.
Free from the fake and phony.
Should I just stay here?
I care to don't care.
Free to scream or a shout.
Should I just get up and go?
Keeping calm in my mind,
I wander about to
feel the touch or, look in one's eyes.
Life...
Experience it.
Embrace it.
Let your emotions be one with you.
Be one with yourself.
All the Walden thinking of you.

Daydream

I walk
with the daisies creeping between my toes,
the sun shining and the sky is so blue.
Calm and quiet,
I walk to shore.
The wind carries my every move.
My toes tickle the water.
My shoulders relax.
I sit and I daydream.
I daydream of wonderful things.
Endless possibilities.
I daydream about me.
I daydream about you.
I daydream about old.
I daydream about new.
And the endless possibilities.
Is it possible to have a limitless ability to love
and dream from within?
Or, maybe this is still just a Daydream?

Calm

Looking at Cloudy days;
and Summer storms,
Love is all I need to stay cool and calm.
Love should be the only
earth-shattering thing to exist.
In this chaotic world, what we need is bliss.

Affirmation

**Always affirm yourself.
There isn't anything wrong with self-
refection or affirmation.
You may or may not get it from others.
Or, just as much as you love others.
Be aware of those
who take more of that and give less back.
Make sure that you remain true and
have your own back.
You will receive the abundance that others lack…
This doesn't always mean in a tangible form.
Affirmations that you give youself
are better than something that can go on your arm.
Love yourself more.
Then the real one will come.**

Hero

Be your own Hero.
You can be what you need for yourself.
Others may not.
They may be un-Balanced.
Trying to achieve a Balance,
without falling from
Yourself,
is a huge, worthwhile journey.

In The Mirror

Looking at me.
Looking at me.
Let's get this understood.
I want to look good.
Because I feel good.
I want to feel good.
Because I look good.
Let's get this understood.
I like to be caressed.
Because I like to be caressed.
I will only do what I want to do.
Let's get this understood.
So,
Baby it is understood.
Dancing, moving and grooving.
This beat got me and my feet
grooving and moving.
Let's get this understood.
I'm going…
And I can't stop!
This is my jam!
This is my shit!
That rhythm!
That groove!
Got me hot!
I'm up out of my shoes!
I will only do what I want to do.
Remember,
we will only do what we want to do!

Love Bonds

Love your family and friends.
Find someone to love and grow together.
Good or bad we all still need love.
We only get one family, or one or two good friends.
Sometimes,
we may add to them;
and other times people have subtracted themselves.
You can love them close or from a distance.
You also have to learn and know them as people.
People may annoy, and at times, avoid each other.
Whomever they are to you,
you can take them or leave them.
But somehow you still love them.

Peace

I hope you find peace and love.
That is the ultimate of riches.
I hope you can navigate life with little to no issues.
For you to live your dreams and invest in your goals.
For you to give and receive the same wonderful love
and energy from others.
I hope you live glorious in this world,
and electrify your soul.

Wonderful

Love should be:
a breath of fresh air and calmness;
the only earth-shattering existence.
Being with someone:
should be everything and blissful;
because you both are wonderful.

Pretty Poetry

While reading a book of poetry,
I like to look pretty.
While still having class,
I like to shake my ass.
When my glass overflows,
I just refill it.
While I like to cloud chase,
I don't clout chase
(for who wants to do that?)
Sometimes, all I want to do is relax.
Chill out and be cozy on my back.
But hey!
How are you?
I'm just being me.
I like to be and have fun.
While continuing being me so naturally.

The Chill Out Mode

Chill out.
Let it out.
Don't worry about any words.
I'll only use them for good.
I'm chilling.
Chill out.
Let it out.
Don't worry about being bored.
I'm a great listener if you have
something good to talk about.
I'm just chilling.
Chill-chill'n out.
Let it out.
I may interject, but no disrespect.
I just want to dwell and relax;
with some fun cool vibes and laughs.
Won't that be great?
Let's make it a date!

Love Self

Come close.
What are my desires?
Do I want mental or physical stimulation?
These feelings are real.
This is not a simulation.
I'm losing breathe.
I'm hot with perspiration.
From looking at myself with admiration.
Damn! I look good.
I feel good too.
Isn't that what self-love is supposed to do?

Interest

Spoken and unspoken inside deep conversations…
Making eye contact;
and already knowing what's up…
"What interests you, my Love?"

Honey Pooh

Ohhhhh, Honey Pooooh...
Breathing deeply; needing to break out.
Bad/Cry/Good/Laugh...
thinking of past times.
Smiling/Smirking/Flirting/Eating…
No love offering unless receiving.
Back hurting from two-sided flirting.
Oh, Honey Pooh what a good night!

Cool to Relate

Can't wait; so ready to go.
Looking good and skin on glow.
I ain't got time to waste.
I like my vodka straight.
I love to eat I'm a foodie.
I like my man with a little bit of weight like me.
It's cool to relate.
But try not to hate.
Close the door.
Shut your mouth.
Told you it was worth the wait.
We are going to party!
Light ups; no fancy cups.
Everyone snacking on chips and dip.
Fresh deck of cards; dominoes, and poker chips.
Dancing and laughter and being carefree.
Old school music never hurt nobody.
I ain't got time to waste.
I like my vodka straight.
I love to eat I'm a foodie.
I like my man with a little bit of weight like me.
It's cool to relate, but try not to hate.
Close the door and shut your mouth.
Told ya it was worth the wait.
We are going to party!
Dance! Dance! Dance!
Dance! Dance! Dance!
Can we all just dance everybody?
We can party without any problems.
Maybe we will all dance our cares away.

Let's dance the night away.
Tonight is a great night to end the day.
Again…
I ain't got time to waste!
I love my man!
I like my vodka straight!
I love to eat;
I'm a foodie!
It's cool to relate!
But try not to hate!
This relationship was worth the wait!
We are going to party!
Oh, no!
Last call!
Hope it was a fun time for all!
Got'ta go and get back.
Join my lover for a nightcap.
But knowing the bonnet's
going on as soon as we get home.
It's okay if ya'll
wanna hang again.
But we've partied out
with good vibes and good people.
It's cool to relate.
Wonder can we do it again like a sequel?
Or, would this time be better or no equal?

Some Men need to be loved too. (Yes)

Hey Babe…
Are you alright?
I will always ask to make sure you are good.
Hey Babe…
What do you need from me?
I will always ask
to make sure your needs and wants are good.
Hey Babe…
You want love from me?
I will always love and kiss on you,
making sure you are good.
Hey Babe...
What is your mood?
I can grab or cook your favorite food.
I am not selfish.
Always, let me know.
Always, let me know.
Always, I will let you know.
Always, I will let you know.
Please, what do I need to do for you?
You deserve it.

Love You

I love you.
Plain and simple.
The words and feelings may seem complex.
At times, it may be hard to express.
(I hope that I say and express it as much).
I love you.
You are a wonderful human being.
I love you.
You are everything.
I love you.
You are strength.
I love you.
You are growth.
I love you.

Open Flower

Let's go to bed together.
Hold each other hands and say our prayers.
Hold each other tight and sleep.
Let's wake up together.
Hold each other tight and talk.
Hold each other's mind at peace.
Let's shower together.
Hold each other under the mist.
Hold each other's hair as we kiss.
Let's have brunch together.
Hold hands and we feed each other.
Hold gazes because we need each other.
Let's do all the things that lovers do.
Let's be all the things that lovers can be.
Let's live the rest of our lives together.

Freaks

Here!
There!
Everywhere!
Hi, there!
Freaks of nature.
It doesn't matter.
Freaks of minds don't mind no time.
Freaks get freaky like the rhythm is shaking them.
Freaking fast or freaking slow.
Keep it moving and out the way!
Freaks ranked in number high or low.
Either way….
(I guess in some ways, we are all some freaks.)

Satin Sheets

Just some satin sheets with me and you.
I want you to meet me in the boudoir.
I got something to show underneath these satin sheets.
Let's love on this bed.
All love goes in deep, love.
All love for the weekend, love.
When you have someone that makes you weak,
change the satin sheets every day of the week.

Again

Kiss me again.
Again, and again.
When you kiss me.
Again, and again.
I want you to hold me.
Again, and again.
When you hold me.
Again, and again.
I want you love on me.
Again, and again.
Until Sunrise.
Then.
Again, and again.
Then you gonna hold me.
Again, and again.
You gonna love on me.
Again, and again.
And always…
Again, and again.
Ooooh make me wet.
Again, and again.
Make me scream out!
Ooooaaawoooah woooahhh
Oooaaaah Ooooaaaawaaah!!!
Again, and again…

So Much More

Love can be so much more than before.
When you open your heart, you can receive love.
Honesty is the closeness of good people.
When you are honest, you can receive good people.
These people can bring the love because they are honest.
They say some people come into your life for a reason.
Does that mean people are just like the seasons?
Love can lead with so much more to explore.
Honesty can lead to much more to learn.
We may never know
who or what they could have meant to us.
Or, what they mean to their world.
Love and openness may not solve much,
but it would do so much more.

We, Love

Thank you for loving me;
and letting me love you.
You are everything.
You are wonderful.
You are magnificent.
You are love.
Oh, baby I love you.
Oh, baby you make love so
sweet; love you so deep.
Come rest in this paradise.
Let me shower you with hugs and kisses.
Still dreaming of you while holding you.
Still feeling all your love inside.
You make me warm and happy.
Always be in love with you,
even when skies are grey.
You are my husband, and my best friend.
I love you.
You love me.
We love we.

Sticky Note Shrapnel

Keep Moving On!
Gotta keep going!
Gotta keep growing!
Ain't no stopping!
Keep on rising!
Trying to be at the top, and party!
Don't test my nature.
What's your vice?
Mines is truth;
self; worth;
and love.
Kee's paper and pen tighter than a glove.
Duo so dope makes the healthiest go ill.
Lyrics can slice,
so sharpen you listening skills.
It thrills us to entertain people with
these rhymes.
No need to check the time;
it's our season, fall back.
Is this all too much?
We'll make you pause; look around;
and ask,"What's up?"

Dazed
(Neil and Charlotte)

Day One

Charlotte Rio opens the computer screen, and taps the START key.
'This was going to be interesting.' she thinks.
Out of curiosity, (or boredom),
Charlotte signed up for a three-day
online seminar for English Literature.
Besides retirement and knitting,
she thinks this continuing education course would be fun.
It may even help with her insomnia.
She enters the meeting ID, and waits for the host to let her in.
Charlotte makes sure her mic is muted; and video is on.
The screen flashes to let her know she is in the seminar.
She adjusts herself and checks her reflection on screen.
Charlotte is glad she is
wearing a nicer red sweatshirt to her outfit.
Good thing they cannot see her leggings.
They are white and red, with reindeer and sleigh bells.
Beep! Beep! Beep!
The screen shows everyone entering.
Boringly, she looks at the it, counting the blocks of people.
So far, only five.
Then she sees someone that catches her attention.
He appears to be around her age,
or a little older; maybe by a couple years or so.
He is wearing a blue sherpa fleece sweater.
His beard is neatly trimmed; his sun kissed skin sets the
contrast to his grey hair
which appears to be pulled back into a ponytail.
'Omg let me not stare.' she thinks.
For some reason, this guy on the screen is so handsome to her.
She turns off her camera.
He, or 'NR363791'. as indicated on his screen, may not
even be around after this,

let alone notice her in a room full of twenty digital people.
The seminar starts; and she is bored.
Looking at the computer's time,
she realizes that not even an hour has passed.
Her mic suddenly jumps on the screen; picking up her yawns.
Good thing she is muted.
NR363791 has turned off his camera.
She turns off her camera and pretends
to listen while her mind daydreams...
Later after the seminar, Charlotte falls asleep for a quick nap.
Late night, she wakes up in the dark condo, hot and horny.
She is feeling a little stress; but somehow, feeling better.
Charlotte is grateful for the long nap.
For some reason, she had a dream about him; NR363791.
'Oh, what a dream!' she thinks.
Slowly, she gathers herself and thoughts on the couch.
After soaking in a bubble bath,
she cooks herself a romantic, candlelit dinner.
As she samples her wine, she wonders about NR363791;
his tastes in music and arts; his career; his everything. She sighs.
Charlotte is not thirsty; but at her age, older,
single people did not have many places to meet
and greet for friendship or a date.
Plus, people are crazy enough so…
After her self-care date,
she treats herself to one of her favorite old movies,
and settles in bed.
Falling asleep,
she starts dreaming about him, hoping to see him tomorrow.

Day Two

The next day she logs on, and turns off her mic and camera.
Charlotte looks at the screen.
NR363791 is not online yet.
Today, she thinks she looks nice.
Charlotte has on her favorite blouse,
a yellow blouse with the magenta hearts;
and a pair of her favorite Lapis Lazuli crystal earrings.
She decides to wear her hair down,
and adds a little lipstick to her normal lip balm routine.
“Why am I doing this?” she says, and laughs out loud.
It is just an online seminar.
‘It’s not like he will see me,’ she thinks.
The screen starts to fill with the participants.
She sees his face pop on the screen.
Her heart skips a beat.
She thinks about her erotic dream last night and blushes.
She pulls herself together
and starts to pay attention to the lecture.
Ten minutes in the seminar,
she receives a private instant message.
‘Hello!’
While she is wondering who could it be,
the person is typing something…
‘OMG that’s him!’
She shakes her head and wonders,
‘Why am I getting nervous?
This is online and we will never meet….
but why am I getting ahead of myself?’
‘Hey!’she types.
Then she deletes it.
She sees he has stopped typing.
Shit, she goes for it!
‘Hello sir’
She types and hits SEND.

'Damn, that was lame.' ponders Charlotte.
Pause…
No response back yet.
She sighs, and gets ready to close the text box.
Ding!
It's NR363791!
'Hey doing well.'
'I didn't see your smiling face today…'
'How are you?' she types back,
'You want to see my smiling face?'
She turns on her camera and smiles.
NR363791 types back.
'You look nice.'
'Thanks; so do you.' she replies.
She turns the camera off before the lecturer notices; and asks Charlotte if she has any questions.
A few more minutes go by.
'This is boring as fuck; I could do better.' he types.
She sends the happy face with tears laughing.
He sends back a meme.
They both LOL on the messages.
Soon they type, 'Goodbye.'
Day two is over.

Day Three

On the last day,
Charlotte logs on earlier than usual.
She wears her favorite purple boucle sweater dress;
cowrie shells and gold beads decorates her now braided hair.
She wears her favorite purple lipstick; and matching eyeshadow.
For pizzazz, she adds silver hoop earrings.
Around ten minutes later, NR363791 logs on.
He looks very refreshing.
Today his hair is down, and is wearing a black tee shirt.
He looks at her and winks.
'Last day!' He types.
'How are you?'
Sighing, she types back,
'IKR. Doing okay.'
They try to listen to the seminar,
but they continue to message each other little jokes and conversations.
Soon the seminar series comes to an end.
NR363791 messages her goodbye.
Charlotte responds the same,
and then gets ready to turn off the lecture.
'Hmm.
The little online crush is over.
It was fun while it lasted…' she thinks.
Ding!
She hears another message.
She is thinking it is the lecturer wanting feedback.
It is NR363791.
'Oh, shit!'
He messaged her his real name and phone number---
with an area code in her city.
Well, okay Neil Maximillian …
She smiles, and replies with her name and number.

Essentially, No Complaints (Victor and Lavender)

Hawthorne Towne Heights Square is slowing down.
Lavender-rose Zeq hopes that she can get her materials
and get home before the weather turns bad.
Generally, she would not work on the weekend.
Six o'clock is the latest you can catch her at the boutique.
The weekend is time for her to relax and retreat,
taking time for herself from work and everyone.
One of the perks of being a small business owner is
that she can set her own hours.
However, since her best friend and business partner,
Kalta Vanguard, had "vanished"
with a pearl farmer, she had to take on more that her
usual share of the business.
Salma Duncan-McPoe, the store's first international
buyer, was traveling to the States Sunday.
Salma wants to purchase some of Lavender's
wearable art pieces, and cashmere fabrics.
Unfortunately, the wintry weather has another plan.
After hours of speaking, Lavender and Salma decide
it is best to have their meeting over video chat;
and Lavender will express mail the order as soon as
the weather clears.
She pulls up to the front of her store and parks her red
sedan in her reserved spot.
As she gets out and walks up to door,
she hears someone call her name.
"Lavender! Lav-en-der!"
'That sounds like Victor.'she thinks, and turns around.
It is Victor.
"Hey, Victor!" she waves.
The gentleman stops a few feet in front of her.
He wore a knitted cap and matching mask, but she still
recognizes his voice.
"Lavender; what's up!
I thought that was you!"
"Yeap it's me," he pulls down his mask to reveal his
signature goatee and smile.

In the 2000s, Victorious "Victor" Edwardson Jr. and
Lavender-rose Zeq attended graduate school together.
After several years, they saw each other again;
but it was to comfort his best friend
Basil about Kalta's disappearance.
When Basil left to get some rest, Victor and Lavender
stayed and talked at her shop; catching up on life.
She laughs and adjusts her handmade purse,
and opens her arms to embrace him.
He smells of a woodsy and masculine cologne.
Victor embraces her back,
inhaling her sweet orchid and lilac fragrances.
"I'm in town to pick up some items from the food market.
I probably will try and catch up with Basil.
I didn't know this was your shop, still."
"Yeah, this is still me.
Well, all me now, since Kalta left," says Lavender.
Victor lets out a low whistle.
"Yea; that's still some wild shit."
"Indeed," she muses.
"Come in."
Lavender gestures towards her shop's sign and unlocks the door.
Victor holds it for Lavender, and they enter the store.
As they take off their coats and shoes, he admires her.
She wears a long sleeve black and white dress
that stops above the knee,
hugging all her thick curves, and leather thigh-high boots.
Lavender's long grey and blue hair
is in waves swept over one shoulder,
revealing her homemade large leather white tassel earrings.
The contrast of the earrings against her butterscotch skin
enhances her natural beauty.
As she puts on her feet a pair of fluffy pink and orange socks,
she catches a glimpse of him looking at her in the huge wall mirror.
She smiles and admires him back.
Victor is wearing a dark green designer sweater;
and dark denim jeans that accent his ass.
Dark green tennis shoes completes his look; and
he is now in his black wool socks only.

At 5’8, Victor is handsome, well-groomed and solid built.
His dark reddish goatee and hair is slightly grey;
the color complementing his medium brown skin.
Lavender walks towards the back of the shop,
and turns on a second light.
“Please, have a seat.”
Near the fabric table, she removes several yards of fabric
from a plush velvet green chair, and gestures for him to sit.
“I just came here to get some fabric samples, and accessories.
A top client was coming by tomorrow.”
“Since the weather is getting bad, we must do a teleconference.”
She goes towards the warehouse area.
“Do you need any help?”
Victor asks as he looks around, still memorized by her work,
and the work of art that he just noticed: her.
“It may be a few rolls and boxes though,” she thinks aloud.
“No problem.”
Rolling up his sleeves,
Victor gets up to follow her to the warehouse.
As they look through the samples and accessories,
they laugh and reminisce about their younger college years.
Holding the red fabric,Victor asks,
“Hey; how come we never dated?”
“Good question. I mean, we did hang out with the same people…”
Lavender looks on the shelf at another sample,
still giving the question more thought.
“You remember the skate party of '08?” asks Victor.
They both start laughing.
“Yes!
I kept falling down because I can’t skate that well.”
Lavender cracks up.
Victor laughs back.
“I know; all night I had to hold your hand around the rink."
"But I didn’t mind it.”
He walks closer to her.
Lavender puts down the fabric.
She turns to him, and they meet eye to eye.
It is no denying the comfort and warmth between them.

It's always been there; but they always denied it.
They inhale each other as they embrace.
She feels him getting slightly hard against her thigh.
He tries to adjust but she pulls him closer.
They lock eyes again.
This means that it is alright.
They start to kiss gently, then more passionately.
Victor and Lavender help each other out of their clothes.
He pulls back; places his hand in his back pocket;
taking out his wallet.
She is familiar with the sound.
He begins to place the protection on.
Not sure of what, why, or which way to go,
she turns and straddles the fabric shelf; granting
Victor more permission.
He slips into her wetness.
She grabs onto the shelves more; trying to steady herself,
and taking in what is all of Victor;
riding the ecstasy wave on his strong, hard dick.
Quiet moans echo the warehouse.
Always the gentleman,
Victor makes sure Lavender gets her first.
"OOOOOOOOOOOOOOOO!"
The sensual movements, and her third,
earth-shattering orgasm rocks the fabric
samples from the shelves.
In perfect harmony, the lovers come.
Like autumn leaves, they fall upon the fabric piles.
A few cling to their sweaty and passion-soaked bodies,
making it appear as if they are a work of art.
They both hold each other amongst
the pink cashmere samples.
"You've…
always…
been beautiful to me…,"
whispers Lavender, rubbing Victor to keep him hard.
"Thanks…
you are beautiful as well,"

he whispers back, putting his fingers in her hair.
Lavender is more than willing and able to return the appreciation.
Slowly, she goes down, placing him in her mouth.
"Oh! Shit!" comes Victor.
And then time stood still...quiet still...
After what seems like a blissful eternity,
Lavender wakes up upon Victor's chest.
He feels her moving to get up, but gently and softly touches her,
bringing Lavender slowly back towards him.
She looks at him, and he smiles and asks,
"Where ya going?"
She smiles and sits up,
rubbing some of the cashmere fabric around her.
Lavender looks at her gemstone watch;
the only thing that is left upon her body.
"It's late; and I need to get these samples..."
She blushes and turns away.
She never thought this would happen with Victor,
or at least not like this.
Essentially, no complaints though.
He notices her smile and reaches out to take her hand.
He kisses it.
"Don't be ashamed now."
They both laugh.
"If anything, it should be me.
How romantic is this," he chuckles.
Victor realizes
that she probably would not be able to sell this fabric.
"Reimburse you?"
He holds up part of the cashmere fabric.
They both laugh.
"No; I'll just make a coat from it; haha."
She turns to rub the silky hair on his chest.
He hugs and holds her, and she does the same to him.
More sleet taps the roof, indicating the nightfall prediction
of wintry weather.

Reluctantly,
the new lovers dress.
After placing a new bundle of cashmere and other fabrics
in a separate box, they prepare to leave the warehouse.
Victor walks her to her car, and places the boxes in her trunk.
"Call you when I make it home?"
She inquires with a huge smile.
"Yes," he responds with the same huge smile.
Victor closes her trunk, and they kiss.
Lavender walks to the sedan's door, and he opens it.
She gets in and they kiss again.
He closes the door, still gazing into her beautiful face.
She gazes and smiles.
"Bye," she rolls up her window, and drives out the parking spot.
He watches her drive off.
Victor heads to his truck; headed back east.
He is excited to see and hear from her later.
As she turns on the highway heading west in her sedan,
she cannot wait to see and hear from him later.
To be continued...

Rediscovery
(Basil and Rika)

Basil

Another sleepless night…
Slowly, Baxterion "Basil" Cunningham opens his eyes,
and sits up on his second-hand vintage California king size bed.
He looks across the room towards the picture window.
The snowy weather makes it hard for him to leave the bed.
Gently, he rests his head against the black marble headboard
that covers most of his light grey accent wall in the grey, white,
and black bedroom of his Hawthorne Towne Estates farmhouse.
'Here we go.' Basil thinks as he swings his legs off the bed.
He slips off his cotton blue boxers,
his manhood slight erect from the erotic dream.
He walks near the glass walk-in closet door,
looks at his reflection, and stretches, trying to relieve some tension.
At 5'7, Basil is a very handsome and striking man.
He keeps his slight salt-and-pepper colored hair cut short,
and his face clean shave.
This makes him look younger than forty-eight.
His milk chocolate skin is smooth like silk, lips nice and kissable.
Long, curly lashes accent dark brown eyes.
Basil does not hear any complaints from the ladies about
himself or manhood.
Some say he was a former 'ladies' man,'
now living the quiet life on a farm.
He wishes he had time to work out or meditate;
but running a business and the food market;
plus, volunteering keeps him in shape and sane.

Yawning and remembering his erotic dream again,
Basil grabs some plush white towels from the linen closet.
He walks into the bathroom and closes the door.
It is time to get started.
Basil dresses in his usual uniform---dark denim jeans and
black tee shirt and socks.
Instead of sneakers, he opts for his black utility boots.
The meteorologist on the small smart television on the wall
speaks of light to moderate sleet.
By Saturday, they mention it will be more extreme weather.
The sun begins to shines; and the wind blows constant chills.
Basil and his dog, Great Puppy, are out the door on time.
He hopes that the weather holds off until he closes the store tonight.
Midwest weather is always unpredictable;
but Midwest-born Basil always enjoys it.
After he graduated from the University and culinary institute,
people could not believe that Basil passed on working with
a renowned chef just to stay in this small town.
He felt that this Towne was a better place for him.
Sometimes, Basil still gets a call or
inquiry about working for Chef Garrett S. DeBon,
but it is always a kind, "No, thank you."
Turning on the radio, Basil settles in for the long 45-minute drive;
trying not to think about Kalta, or his erotic dream.

Rika

Rika Maximillian-Duncan used to hate getting up early.
Now she appreciates the morning's glory and beauty.
Downtown Hawthorne Towne Heights Square
will be bustling soon enough,
and she likes to take the town's quiet time to reflect and create.
Today, for some reason,
she wakes up thinking that a walk/run will help clear her mind.
After making her bed,
she heads towards the shower with no time to waste.
As of now,
Rika is the new owner of the towns only
vintage antique and furniture shop.
It is a quick life turn, but hey, she enjoys it.
She needed to move to this small-town,
especially after what happened in Rome.
Winston…
the incident…
the pool table downstairs…
all memories she is trying to forget.
Coming back here is her recharging and rediscovering herself.
Stepping out the shower,
she dries herself off with a fluffy yellow bath towel.
At 5'4', Rika is an everyday beauty; even though she
begs to differ with modesty.
With a heart shaped face, skin the color of sepia; hazel eyes,
and luscious lips, she is a quite beauty.
At first, Rika did not understand her unique beauty.
Being older made her appreciate and love herself more.
She feels most beautiful and comfortable in her mid-forties;
and being in her 'soft-era'.
She did not mind her slight tummy,
generous bosoms, booty, and thighs.
Her raven-colored hair is longer than before;
now it reaches pass her waist.

Winston will not like it; he once said she looked too bohemian;
but she did not care.
Walking towards the 1980s white shabby chic dresser with mirror,
she repeats her naked affirmations.
Humming and trying to keep it peaceful,
she gathers her purple athletic undergarments and white socks
from the dresser drawers, and purple jogging suit from nearby closet.
Careful not to disturb her sore knee, Rika sits on her bed and dresses.
Tying her orange running shoes laces, she gets off the bed.
It creaks just like left knee.
The bed is very vintage; but with a new mattress set.
Thank goodness for the new mattress, especially for these last sleepless;
loveless nights.
She had not planned to stay in the store's upstairs loft long.
However, after the divorce is final from Winston, she is
staying longer.
This town has always been her earthly comfort blanket;
and now, she is so in love with it.
Every summer or holiday festival,
Rika and her family would visit Grandfather at his farm estates.

For over 32 years,
Professor Walton Neil Maximillian IV,
or, Neil as they affectionately call him,
owned, 'Maximillian's Vintage and Second-Hand Antiques.'
Recently, he decided to retire from teaching, and the shop.
Neil fell in love with Charlotte Rio.
They met online at a seminar,
fell in love; and decided to travel world.
When Grandpa called and offered his favorite granddaughter
the shop and loft, Rika did not hesitate to accept.
A month or so ago, before Winston returned from his trip
to Australia, Rika left Rome; heading back to the Midwest.
She shakes her head, trying to get herself together.
She makes a mental food list.
After the run, she will stop by 'Quinoa Oasis,'
and grab some groceries, or one of those
fresh prepared homemade dinners.
Rika is tired of eating fast food,
and her squash is getting low.
She has wine and hot and spicy chips,
so she did not have to go to the city for better snacks.
Rika bounces down the back loft steps
and towards the front door of the shop.
She grabs her heavier jacket of the 1920s coat rack.
The weather feels less windy, but the winds would pick up soon.
Who knows; it may pass the town over,
but they say be prepared.
She wonders if she will ever be prepared for this
Midwest weather again.
She only misses Rome's weather somedays,
but loves a good snowstorm.
Locking the door, Rika heads to the trail.

Basil

'Quinoa Oasis' is located near the downtown area of
Hawthorne Towne Square Heights.
Along this newly renovated strip mall is
the winding trail of the Whitman Fields Nature Reserve Park.
Basil's store shares the strip with a novelty shop;
a bookstore; "The Gallery;"
a jewelry/art boutique,
and the newly renovated indoor/outdoor skating rink.
Across the street is a newly opened spa and mediation center;
a vintage secondhand antique furniture shop; and a
burlesque theater.
Basil pulls up to the parking lot he shares with bookstore.
Rolling up the windows on black his pickup truck,
he briefly sees a thick figure standing the across the street.
Curious, he watches her as she turns and pulls
the heavy door of the antique shop close.
Pulling her hair into a loose bun,
she turns and runs, her orange reflector running shoes lighting up.
'This must be Rika.' he thinks.
Professor Walton Neil Maximillian IV had asked his
former student, Basil
to reintroduce himself to his granddaughter, Rika.
But Basil had been too busy with payroll to attend
the town's welcome party for her at, 'The Gallery.'
Although not afraid of Neil,
Basil is cautious of meeting Rika again.
When she was in town, it was normally for
a few weeks in the summer, or during the busy shopping season.
He knows how much Neil loves his grandchildren, Rika, and Taal.
Taal Maximilian is twelve years older than Basil; and
attended school with Basil's older brother, Mayson.
Taal is married and lives with his wife, Rainney at
the Maximillian Family Farm Estates.

He only knew that after college, Rika became a stay-at-home wife to the arrogant Winston McKane Duncan, heir and owner of McKane Duncan Property Appraisals, a worldwide renowned prestigious appraisal management corporation.
The small town's talkers are whispering and wondering why spoiled Rika Maximilian-Duncan suddenly moved from her rich extravagant life in Rome back to this sleepy, dark town.
Who would leave that luxury
lifestyle to supervise and live over a vintage shop?
Some of the business owners worry about McKane Duncan Property Appraisals coming there to buy other properties.
'Hmm…'
Basil thinks as he watches her turn and jog down the Trail.
She has a nice small-town shape---healthy and thick.
Great Puppy barks, bringing Basil back to reality.
He laughs and proceeds to let them truck.
They both head towards the store to start the workday.

Rika

The sunrise indicates that the trail is open.
Rika only has a few minutes before the town wakes up.
Normally, she leaves out the side door,
but since the time has not changed, and the backdoor is
near the community pond where the wild ducks live,
she feels more comfortable going out
the store's front door.
As soon as she steps outside, and locks the heavy antique door,
she hears the familiar sound of tires rolling down the road.
It must be Basil.
Some reason, her heart flutters.
From younger years of visiting her grandfather and cousins,
she would see Basil, but from afar.
Her brother Taal attended high school with Basil's older
brother, and mayor of Hawthorne Heights, Mayson.
When they were younger, she thought
Basil was finer than the other Cunningham men.
Every time she goes to the store for a few items,
either he is remarkably busy,
or talking with the Legacy Women, who are always thirsty for
him, flirting and breasts all in his face.
Town gossip is that he either has a girlfriend
or ex-fiancée that is missing at sea.
She hears the truck turn off.
Slowly, she turns around and starts to jog in place.
She hears the window roll up,
and Basil steps out the truck with his dog.
She sees the curvature of his body.
'Healthy foods make a body and a butt good.' she muses.

Feeling herself grow warm,
she places her earbuds in her ears
and starts to jog towards the trail...
Day turns into night.
The sky starts to cloud up, indicating what storm is to come.
"Thank goodness it's the weekend!"
Vicky Bender is the only other employee of the shop.
Her and her husband are longtime friends of Neil and the family.
"Yes; indeed, here we are…
another weekend…," murmurs Rika.
She is ready for the day to end, but knew she will
be going back upstairs to bed; to snuggle with a delightful book,
and turn on a reality show for conversation.
The sweet and mild aromatic smells
of the French onion soup in the slow cooker wafts
from the kitchen and into the room.
"Food smells good," mentions Ms. Vicky.
She has on her coat, and stands by the door,
waiting patiently for her husband to arrive. "Shit!
I forgot to go into the city for French bread!" Rika exclaims.
It is too late to drive to the city.
She needs her carbs.
If need be, she will have to make do without it.
"Well, why don't you go across the street to Basil's
and get some bread?
He has more healthy selections anyway.
Me and Mr. B. buy from his bakery all the time.
Exceptionally good."
"You know what; maybe.
I have been too busy to go over and talk to him.
Taal told me to be nice; you know;

try to get out; and not be so consumed with work.
I mean Basil and I knew each other from back when
we used to visit Grandfather here."
"Hmm...
Now I do think it may do you some good;
to make new friends," Ms. Vicky says, as she grabs
her magenta wool scarf and matching hat
from the 1920s cast iron coat rack.
"That Basil is a handsome man.
Too bad about him and his ex..."
"Well, you may want to go now;
looks like the everyone is closing shop."
"I'll walk out with you."
Rika grabs her lilac jacket and slips
her feet into a pair of black leather sneakers by the door.
"Okay, let's go.
You need to be back here in 20 minutes.
Now don't let me have to call and check on ya,"
Ms.Vicky smiles, and hugs Rika.
Rika appreciates it.
Ms. Vicky and her husband have always been like
an aunt and uncle to her.
Honk! Honk!
Mr. Zeppie K. Bender always pulls up the shop's door.
He parks and steps out to open the door for her.
After 51 years; 7 children; and
over twenty grand and great
grandchildren, they still have that love and fire for each other.
"Hey, Rika!
How do you do today?"
Mr. Bender waves to her as he closes Ms.Vicky's door.
"Doing well, Mr. Z!," she waves back.
"Have a good evening!"
Ms.Vicky waves and they drive off,
happily talking about something.
Rika thinks to herself about how she thought she had that love...
and about the love that was taken from her...
She hears the old grandfather clock in the corner.
The clock strikes 8:00 pm.
The store closes at 9:00 pm.
She proceeds to grab her tote bag, and
quickly head across the street to the store.

Basil

Before Basil knows it, the day turns into night.
Upstairs in his office, he hears the wind picking up.
Most of the building owners use their space as storage
but he converted the space into an office,
keeping the same architectural structure and style.
Over the years, most of the furniture he bought
came from the vintage or second- hand stores.
He turns around in his vintage office chair, and
looks out his picturesque office window.
Downstairs, the bustle of people has stopped.
Basil gets up and heads downstairs
to let the last employees go home early.
He is about to lock up the market area
when he hears a slight pull on the door.
Looking up, Basil sees Rika at the door.
She smiles and waves at him.
Basil walks to the door and unlocks it.
“Thanks!"
"Is it too late to get some artisan bread or quick items?
Since the weather is turning bad, and I did not have time to
make a special trip into town…”
She steps inside the doorway.
Her raven-colored hair is wet from light snow;
her face looks cute and dewy.
“Hey!
Is it okay if I grab a few items?” she inquires again.
“Sure,” Basil says as he closes and locks the door.
Looking at her reflection from the door’s window,
he is slightly memorized.
He cannot remember her ever looking this pretty.

Breathing slowly,
Basil turns the sign to 'Closed' and proceeds to walk with Rika.
"Produce or bakery?" he asks as he touches her arm slightly.
Even with the wintry weather, he feels her warmth.
"Bakery, please."
"I need some carbs,
and that delicious organic coffee creamer," she adds.
"Coming right up,"
Basil hands her the last of the freshly baked bread;
adding some additional fresh baked pastries.
"Thanks!"
Rika carries the basket towards the counter, ready to pay.
"No payment necessary.
This is on the house."
"What…oh, thank you!
That is too kind," she blushes.
"And, you added extra pastries; and you need your money…"
"Let's go out tomorrow night… "
blurts out Basil.
"I mean, if the weather is nice, would you like to go to the bistro for an early dinner?"
"Plus, I did not get a chance to formally reintroduce myself,
per Neil's instructions."
'Maybe it will help me forget about Kalta.' he thinks.
Rika laughs; for that sounds like her grandpa.
"Sure; I'd like that."
'Basil is so handsome;
why had she not notice this more than before?
And, it would be nice to forget about Winston for a moment.'
thinks Rika. "Great. Pick you up around 6:30 pm?" Basil asks.
"Yes," she replies, her smile bigger.
Rika is eager with interest.
After closing up the store and market,
and seeing Rika safely cross the street and enter her shop,
Basil goes upstairs to his private office suite/loft.
He gathers his belongings;
whistles for Great Puppy, and walks downstairs to go home.

Dinner

Saturday night is here.
A light sleet is falling now, but ice is expected later.
They hope to have a quick dinner, and Basil
can head home before the roads are due to close.
If not, he may have to spend the weekend in his office.
After a relaxing shower,
Basil gets ready for his date with Rika.
Wearing a plain black collar shirt, denim jeans;
and grey tennis shoes,
he grabs his navy suit jacket and cowboy hat,
and leaves the Farm.
Again, he is excited to see Rika...
At the shop, Rika paces slightly to the door anticipating Basil's
arrival. She glances at herself in the 18th century
stained-glass floor-length mirror.
A red denim fedora covers her long hair.
She wears a neon green scarf over a grey turtleneck; a
leopard print skirt; lace tights; and designer combat boots.
For accessories, she wears her
favorite gemstone bracelet and earrings.
The wind again the window
tells her that the weather is turning up quick.
A weird feeling of wonderment tickles at her heart.
What happens if he cancels?
She will not be surprised.
Even she has yet to get use to the Midwest winters.
The doorbell chimes.
She grabs her long denim coat and matching purse.
As soon as she picks up her cellphone from the pool table…
BEEP. BEEP. BEEP.
Unknown number.
This is the fifth time today.

‘Gotdamn.’
She shakes her head.
She puts the phone on silent and tosses it into her purse.
Then she opens the door.
Basil is here with flowers, and eager to see her, too...
Luckily for them, the café is slightly emptied.
They find a booth by the bamboo trees in back corner.
He helps Rika out of her coat, and into the booth; then
sits on the opposite side, facing her.
Besides the soft background music,
their laughter and conversation fill the smooth and quiet
atmosphere of the café.
The gold chandelier and string
lights above their heads gives them an ethereal like glow.
They order dinner.
When it is served, it mostly goes untouched...
The snow is not the only thing that is getting heavy.
Basil and Rika now sit closer; conversation more intimate.
The new friends are open about their past, present, and future.
Basil opens up to Rika about his ex-girlfriend, Kalta,
running off with a pearl farmer.
Since Kalta vanished four years ago,
Basil says he is either busy or by himself.
Sometimes, he hangs out with his best friends:
Victor, from college; and Leo and Summer,
his married friends, that own and operate
'The Gallery,' not too far from ‘Quinoa Oasis.’
Kalta Vanguard once collaborated with her best friend,

Lavender-rose Zeq at the boutique adjacent to,
'The Gallery.'
He is heartbroken; but he always felt that they
were heading towards a breakup.
“OMG;
I thought that was just a rumor,”
exclaims Rika, upset with emotions.
‘Why would someone leave a wonderful man
like Basil Cunningham?’ she wonders.
‘She must be a fool.’
“Well; if this makes you feel any better,
I caught my soon-to-be ex-husband,
Winston having a secret rendezvous with one of his employees.
In case you have not notice, he is the
‘McKane Duncan’ in 'McKane Duncan Property Appraisals.'
“Wow; and now I’m sorry to hear that.”
Just like Rika, Basil’s emotions fill with concern.
“I can’t believe he would do that.
What an arrogant piece of shit.”
‘She is just too good for him.’ Basil thinks.
“I heard he came to town last year; trying to
appraise properties or something?”
Basil inquires trying
not to be angry at some dude he did not know.
Rika sighs.
“Something to that nature; but only the Shop;
and Grandfather said he would never sell it.”
“Good for Neil.
It's strange that Winston would want to appraise the shop.
I mean; this is his wife’s family legacy."
“Right,” she agrees.
“Guess we both have had some strange relationships,”
half jokes Basil.
They both laugh.

"K-I-S-S. I love it when you R-I-D-E on me…."
croons the soulful song on the jukebox.
The night moves in moments of stimulating conversations,
peaceful glances, and foot rubbing.
By now, Basil and Rika know what is to come next.
They agree to spend the night together.
"If it's alright with you," Basil ask, standing to help
Rika with her coat.
"May I come back to your loft?
I would like to finish this debate on
lemon meringue pie versus chocolate mousse cake."
Basil knows he can spend the night upstairs in his
store's office/loft, but he is enjoying this lady; her aura;
and their conversations.
Rika blushes "Sure; I would like that;
but the weather is bad…
shouldn't you…"
Basil places his fingertips on Rika's lips.
"Shh…," he looks into eyes.
She kisses his fingertips.
"Okay…" she grabs her purse.
They head out the bistro, almost leaving the food.
"Hey, don't forget the food!" the door attendant, Rafeal,
who is waiting for his rideshare,
calls after them, holding their brown bag of food.
Giggling like secret lovers,
Basil grabs the food from him.
He holds the door open for Rika,
and they carefully walk to 'Quinoa Oasis.'

The cold, bitter wind is winding,
but the hot passionate soon to be lovers do not notice.
Basil needs to get his overnight duffel bag from the his store.
Inside of the ‘Quinoa Oasis’ window,
the dog is sitting in his kennel by the door.
“Oh, is it okay that I bring my dog, Great Puppy?
If not, it’s cool; I can…”
Basil voice trails off.
“Yes; I would love to see Great Puppy.
I have the perfect space for him as well,” she speaks.
Basil lets her inside of the store.
She goes towards the Labrador’s kennel.
The dog beckons for her to unlock it.
She does, and he jumps on her, giving a warm, puppy love hug.
“Hey,” Rika smiles.
“Hey, Great Puppy.”
“Down, boy,” gently Basil commands the dog.
Basil has returned with his duffle bag,
thinking that Great Puppy may be too friendly for Rika.
"If Great Puppy likes you, he will jump on you for a hug."
“Oh, he is a good dog,” says Rika as she stands up.
“I love that name.”
Great Puppy goes to the kennel and gets in.
“Come on Great Puppy; you’re coming with us,” laughs Basil.
The dog barks in agreement; making them laugh.
Basil always knew that Great Puppy could get
a pretty lady to laugh.
Turning off the lights, and setting the alarm, they proceed to
leave the store...
The snow continues to blanket the earth.
Most of the Square’s business
are closed; and people are slowing driving away towards the city.
Carefully, Basil, Rika, and Great Puppy cross the street to the shop.
Once inside,
Rika motions for Basil and the puppy to get comfortable.
“Take a look around;
I’ll be back in a moment, Great Puppy can go in
the second room on the left.” says Rika.
Next to the doorway that Rika enters, there stands an old jukebox;

and several albums; and a nice oak wood pool table.
Basil notices the pool table.
He realizes how much this little shop is full of treasures.
A pool table is on his wish list for his recreational basement.
'Rika just may have a buyer for this one.' he thinks.
In bold red letters, "$5500 or best offer," reads on the sign.
Little did he know
the pool table is one of the few items she did want to sell.
The quicker she sells this 1978 classic, the better.
Funny, she has not had any offers on that table.
Walking towards the table,
Basil asks, "Do you play?"
Rika laughs from the kitchen.
"No; but it brings back good and bad memories.
One, this table was a wedding gift to me and Winston…"
She pauses not sure if she should mention
that they once made passionate love there,
no longer making her a virgin bride.
"I'm getting us some tea," Rika changes the subject.
"That sounds good," he says.
He wonders why she wants to sell it; but who would
want to keep a wedding gift if you are getting a divorce?
"Maybe, one day I could teach you how to play.
That is, if you decide to keep it for entertainment
purposes," jokes Basil as he is picking up one of the pool sticks.
"I'm not much of a player; but it would be cool to learn how,"
laughs Rika from the kitchen.

She comes back with a marble tray and matching marble
teapot and cups.
The smell of green tea with ginseng and honey wafts in the air.
"Thank you."
Basil walks closer, to help her with the tray.
He stands gently in front of Rika.
His breath is peaceful against her face
as he reaches for the marble tray.
Basil being so close to her makes her
feel something wonderful in her breast.
She feels her nipples go hard.
'Damn,
I'm wearing the wrong bra, too lacey!' she thinks.
'Such a gentleman she thought;
if he did see, he didn't embarrass me.'
She is now comfortable again.
And, that is all it takes.
She is hot… so hot she almost splashes them both with the tea.
"What do you like?"
Basil is trying to keep calm.
He takes the tray from her
and places it on the redwood dining table.
He looks at her.
She is so
beautiful.
Her shape is a song of cuddliness and comfort.
Basil has been celibate for four years…
but something about her makes him want to come undone.

Although did not assume they will be intimate, he is
glad he tossed a fresh pack of protection in his duffelbag.
Not saying he was going to get any from this lovely Rika.
From the universe, and for some reason; the aura and
chemistry are electric.
The new friends settle on the leather sofa, and sip tea,
talking about their favorite movie adaptation of a classic novel.
Stretching his legs, Basil gets up and walks around the shop.
He has always admired the shop;
but appreciates it now that he is older and a collector of finer things.
Across the room against the burgundy painted accent wall,
stands a gigantic, green, and gold trimmed antique mirror.
He gravitates towards the tall mahogany bookcase
full of vintage records, albums and cassettes.
He walks over to the matching table and picks up the glass lid
of the 1980s style stereo console made from precious
metal trim and oak wood.
The sign says that only two are made in the country,
but it is not for sell.
Neil loves that stereo. However, against Neil and Rika's wishes,
Winston has appraised it for $92,000.
Rika walks towards the mirror and looks at herself.
Basil watches her reflection.
She sees him and smiles back.
Gingerly, Basil picks two albums from center shelf;
'KDLPC's Lounge Style,'
and a classic seventies soft yacht rock compilation.
"Wow; I had this compilation back in the day."

"Yes;
I still love it.
It's a classic; so is anything
'KDLPC,'" Rika says with a smile.
"I may need to check them out."
Basil pulls the album from the 'KDLPC' cover sleeve.
Rika wishes he pulls something else out for her.
'Can't help it; I gotta a dirty mind.
I know the attraction is there.
Let the universe work.' she thinks and laughs aloud.
Curious as to why she is laughing, he gazes at her,
smiles; and places the album on the turntable.
Softly, the music drifts around them.
As she reaches to braid her hair,
Rika slowly starts to arch her back and wine towards Basil.
They both start to dance and sway.

Wet

Close they move with each other, feeling warm and
wet for each feel.
Realizing that are now slow grinding and
kissing, Basil politely lets her go,
and readjusts himself, and then her skirt.
But, she moves closer and starts to grind on him more.
They kiss.
He accepts this offer and starts to rub her backs
degingerly, trailing down to her soft and supple ass.
Slowly, Rika starts to melt.
She has never felt like this… ever?
Long time? Really?
'Oh, fuck it!' she thinks.
'Or, me.'
'Or, him….'
From all the dancing and grinding,
they find themselves back by the pool table.
They start to undress each other.
Pausing,
Basil goes to retrieve the fresh
golden packets from his overnight bag.
Although celibate, he stills travels with them.
Rika sees and appreciates him immediately.

Then she sees his hard, large thickness
and almost loses her breathe.
This will be the only second but to none other.
She is ready and hot.
And, she wants him now.
After placing the rubber on,
he turns back to her, politely asking her,
“Where do you want it?”
‘She is a lady; I will always ask.’ he thinks.
'This is a first; his is a gentleman lovemaker;
Winston is a selfish lover.’ she thinks.
“How do you want it?”
"Give it to me like you want it…" she breathes.
He never had permission granted before.
Mostly, Kalta was a selfish lover.
“Are you sure?”
She gasps,
“Yes,” and grabs his dick.
He slips his fingers inside of her.
Adoringly, he bends her over the left pocket corner
of the billiard table.
She grasps and spreads wider, taking the tip in slowly.
Slowly and gently,
Basil enters her; making sure not to hurt her.
He assures her not to worry.

She is able to take it all in her wetness.
Moans of pleasures echo the room.
Quickly, the lovers get their synchronization.
"Damn you....
You feel....
feel good!"
"You...
do...
too... ooooo!"
Moans of lovemaking
create a wonderful melody for the music lovers.
The waves and rhythm continue to rise.
He licks her earlobe.
She squeezes her hips and legs in response.
As gentle as the snowfall on the nearby mountain top,
the newly minted lovers reach their peaks.
Slightly breathless, Basil and Rika slowly stand up.
She turns to look at him eyes filled with
extraordinary pleasure.
He returns the look just as eager and hungry for more.
Taking hands, they both proceed upstairs to the bed.

More Loving

Sensually kissing and touching, they enter the bedroom,
and fall upon the queen size bed covered with purple
and gold satin sheets.
Getting comfortable amongst the pillows,
Basil proceeds to lay Rika on her backside and starts to kiss
and lick her from head to middle to toe,
to the middle, resting in her waterfall of loveliness.
Afterwards, Rika returns the pleasure
of gliding her tongue upon the smooth,
silky and shiny essence of a man that was
much more than she had ever taken in.
Then they both pleasure each other in a range of styles
of lovemaking positions ever known to most confident lovers.
They both lose count of their screaming passions.
The new lovers hold each other, drifting off to a
deep nice slumber, much needed for two whom once lacked sleep,
and the comfort of being held by someone just as special.

The Weekend, Love (Again)

Like silk thread through gemstones,
Saturday's late night slips into a very early Sunday morning.
Its sunrise cascades through the silk green and purple paisley
royal Victorian curtains hanging on the bay windows.
Cardinal birds harmonize in their birdhouse
by the blossom trees; singing a song of newfound love.
The tree has grown to a nice shade tree throughout the years.
Its bare fingers tickle the windows of Rika's loft,
as if to gently awake the lovers...
Quietly, Rika and Basil slow stir in the bed.
She rolls towards him.
He feels her and gets slightly hard.
"Good morning, sunshine," he kisses her bare neck,
adding a little tip of his tongue.
"Good morning, sunshine," she moans back,
arching her back in a sexual stretch.
She is ready for more passion…
Vroom!
Vroom!
Vroom!
"Who is that?"
Basil whispers as he keeps Rika closer.
"I do not know."
She tenses up a little;

upset by the interruption,
but curious about why that strange number keeps calling.
“This weird ass number has been calling me."
“Scam?”
“Not sure,” Rika replies.
“But it shows up private or no ID.”
“Well, you could the cell company to see who it could be;
that may help,” mentions Basil as he rubs her backside.
“I should, but this is a new number.
Once Winston and I started the divorce,
I changed my number.”
She rolls around in the bed to face Basil again,
and props upon one of the satin pillows.
He pulls her close, and they kiss with simmering passion.
Downstairs, the dog begins to bark.
“In a moment,
I will take Great Puppy outside; then head to the store.
Afterwards, I will come back;
feed us; and we can ravish each other again.”
“And, again,” she flirts, rubbing manhood back hard.
“Aaaaaaa….” he moans in response.
“Yes; again...”
After another quickie,
the lovers hold each other and talk about Poe.
Lovingly, Rika looks at Basil as he gets ready to
head out with Great Puppy.
She feels a slight waterfall build in her garden again.
He kisses her and gets out of bed.

Basil stands, and the sunlight outlines the firmness
and curves of his marvelous body.
Even from his side profile, he is a man that carries
one of the longest, thickest,
and heaviest sticks she had ever imagined, no comparison.
'From A-Z; that man is everything marvelous.' she thinks.
Downstairs, Great Puppy starts to bark again.
"Menu ideas for brunch?" Basil yawns, and smiles.
"We already have dessert covered," she jokes.
They both smile at each other.
"Brunch. Lunch. Dessert…love making..." grins Basil.
"Yes, to all three,"
Rika moans and rolls back on the satin sheets,
as she watches Basil put on his grey sweatsuit and tennis shoes.
He blows a kiss to her.
"Get some rest.
I will be right back."
"Sounds wonderful," she says, pulling up the covers,
trying to rest her aching back. Basil heads downstairs to start the day.
By the secret side door,
he grabs a brown hoodie from the coat rack.
"Here, Great Puppy."
With Great Puppy by his side, his unlocks the door and steps out.
Stuffing his hands in his pockets to
keep warm, he is pulls out a surprise.
He does not remember the rollie and lighter from last night,
but he remembers their already deep,
intellectual and sexy conversation,

and chemistry, elevated to even more intellectual
and sexually heights once this was incorporated.
'Rika could be the one.'
He thinks takes a puff.
'Wow.'
After Great Puppy finishes his business,
Basil and the dog proceed to walk to 'Quinoa Oasis.'
Odd to him, he hears what sounds like a vehicle
coming down the frosted road.

Winston

The road closure did not stop him from coming.
As the shiny black, tinted windows luxury vehicle descends the narrow road,
the driver looks in the mirror towards his godson.
"Ready?" the chauffeur asks.
"Ready," his godson replies; a little nervous.
For so long, this moment has been on his mind.
Slowly, the chauffeur pulls the vehicle up and parks in front of Maximilian's.
The elderly driver,
dressed in a dark navy-blue suit and overcoat,
gets out and opens the back door for the passenger.
A medium height, solid stature man steps out.
His hair is straight and reddish black and pulled back in a long ponytail.
He wears a long wool camel colored plaid overcoat, over a three-piece tailored suit.
His necklace bears three huge wedding bands.
In his brown leather gloved hands, he holds a bouquet of flowers, and his hat.
Placing his dark green cowboy hat on his head, the man deeply inhales and exhales.
Winston McKane Duncan was back in town.
He is here to claim what is rightfully his.
He is here to rediscover his wife.

To be continued ….

(Bonus Words)
Keestyle

Just because someone has felt or experienced
your same pain does not mean that the person will
or has to place that pain on you.
It's alright to talk about,
but don't revisit the conversation in anger or deflection.

About the Author Kalisha D. Lemmitt-Cherry
Author, editor, producer, artist, and songwriter.
Born and raised in Saint Louis, MO,
Kalisha has obtained a Bachelor of Arts in English;
Certificate in Creative and Technical Writings
(University of Missouri-Saint Louis, 2007);
Master of Education in Adult and Higher Education and
(University of Missouri- Saint Louis, 2010).
In 2000, she started fmentoring; freelancing and tutoring.
In 2008, she cofounded member of "KDLPC."
with Peter Cherry.
Kalisha is Owner and CEO at 'Serenity Writing and Editing Services, Inc' (2011); and COO, 'Angelic Reign Inc.' (2016).

We are KDLPC: Kalisha L. Cherry & Peter Cherry

Angelic Reign Inc. Presents:

We got Books & Music,
Music & Books,
along with Artwork.
More to come....

The Bonus Flow

Weep

It was done.
I won for me.
But, why is it so bittersweet?
Alone, I feel.
Alone, I weep.
For this is all bittersweet.
No fanfare for me.
No prizes for me.
Just selfishness.
Oh, so selfish people.
Yes, the melancholy is getting
a hold of me.
Yes, it is finally done.
I'd thought I won one;
just unselfishly, for myself.
Yes, it is done; but it is
bittersweet, and, alone I
feel and weep.

Cold

In the house looking;
through a window pane.
I've locked my doors.
It's cold and I'm old.
I've got my blankets and cocoa.
Watching the squirrels gather nuts,
while they have a look of disdain and,
'what the fuck' looking back at me.

Insomnia, Too

Mad, indeed I am.
I should be asleep.
But, I'm up.
I'm still writing with a pen, and on
paper.
I haven't slept in days.
My insomnia has kicked in.
My skin is
Lavender scented, but my mind
is slight demented.
Yet, had to finish
this book...

Leggings

We're at home.

We're comfortable.

I put my leggings on; my leggings on;
my leggings on.
I'm putting my leggings on; taking off my
bra; putting on one of your old t-shirts;
putting my hair up; and grabbing a book.
Chilling and relaxing with
you, as we talk and you cook.

Is This You?

Who you really are?
Is this who are you really?
Who is you really?
Who are you really are?
Is this who you really are to you?

Facts

Tired of it seeming like we are going tit for tact.
When, in fact, we are saying similar facts.
All I'm trying to do is show you where I'm at.
Because I've been there before.
Sometimes,
I've already had done that.
I'm being inclusive in the conversation.
Not being intrusive of your situation
or thoughts.
But hey, it works both ways.
Either,
I stay quiet and listen,
or let you know
I can or cannot relate.
But you can't get mad with
the facts.

Situation

It's a sticky situation;
and we got to handle it.
It's a sticky situation;
and, we said we will handle it.
Let's not struggle.
Let's not argue.
Let's continue
to get better.
And, break the cycles.
No; struggle love is not welcomed here.
Let's not continue the bullshit.
This pull-and-tug.
We ain't going to war.
Too great of a love that we have for us collectively,
and, for you and me, individually.
Not going to bed mad.
Never eating alone.
Let's break the cycle,
and neither leave communication
nor conversations unspoken.

Get Down

Heaviness..
I need to dance!
Where is my crown?
I came here to get down.
I didn't come here to see you frown.
I came here to get down.
I don't wanna be down on my luck.
I don't wanna be down in the dumps.
I don't wanna be down; down; down; down; down.
Where I can't get up;
get it up; up; up; up and dance.
Where is the groove?
I came here to get down;
get down; get down; get down.
Dance and groove here is
all I came to do.
With my crown,
I came here to
get down.

No

I don't want to be a
human being in perpetual
sadness or madness.

Get Through

Love is all we need
to get through the seasons; give reason
for hope, and a good, wild time.

Sweet

I'm just sweet.
Sweet.
I love life and living it.
The places I go; people I meet.
Sometimes,
I may be goody or moody.
But I am always keeping it sweet.
I'm just
sweet;
sweet;
sweet.

Shh!

When I wanted to talk,
your silence was golden.
Now, I've chosen
to grow.
Now, I know
my closure came
from the within myself.
Not sure where
this leaves you at.

Growing

It still hurts;
it just hits different
in its way.
Don't get in your way of growth,
or let anyone else do so.
See and embrace the growth in you;
and then you can see and embrace it
all around.

True

-but some people you can't please
Me-but in my mind I'm okay
-but some things you can't change
Me-but in my truth I'm good

Easy

Sometimes,
the word is hard;
and my thoughts are ajar.
But, do we all know oneself?
Is it okay to ask for help?
Love someone in life and death?
Why be mean?
I'm trying to live out the rest of
life nice, loving, and easy.

Expire

The time has expired
I'm not talking to you,
I'm moving higher,
Not going lower.
The time has expired.
I'm moving higher.
Not going lower for ya.

Note to Reader

From here, to
there, and
almost everywhere;
thank you for visiting and taking
this journey with me.
The Past;
Present; and future,
I will always see you again.

Thank You

Thanks and Love to God.
All things and more are possible.
Thanks and Love to my
Family; and those who
care; who are gone; and who
are still here.
Thank you, and Love you, Peter.
Thank you, and Love you, Me.

Purse design by Kalisha D. Lemmitt-Cherry

Together: By Kalisha D. Lemmitt-Cherry

Purse designs by Kalisha D. Lemmitt-Cherry

www.ingramcontent.com/pod-product-compliance
Lightning Source LLC
LaVergne TN
LVHW090613110826
845146LV00001B/371

* 9 7 9 8 9 9 0 2 5 7 8 3 2 *